NO WAY OUT
BUT THROUGH

PITT POETRY

50 YEARS

SERIES

Ed Ochester, Editor

NO WAY OUT
BUT THROUGH

Lynne Sharon Schwartz

University of Pittsburgh Press

Published by the University of Pittsburgh Press, Pittsburgh, Pa., 15260
Manufactured in the United States of America
Printed on acid-free paper
10 9 8 7 6 5 4 3 2 1

ISBN 13: 978-0-8229-6459-9
ISBN 10: 0-8229-6459-7

Cover photo © Rachel Schwartz
Cover design by Melissa Dias-Mandoly

CONTENTS

One

Veronica Lake   5

Collecting Myself   6

The Ladders   7

Nocturnal Repertory   8

Forgetting   10

First Loves   11

Hard and Soft   14

What the Poets Never Write about Love   15

The German Class   16

Namesake   17

A Dress Laments   18

A Bad Rap   20

The Two Supers   21

Renée Returned   22

Trans   24

Stitching Skin   25

Two

For Beverly

Reduced   29

No Way Out but Through   30

Dayyenu   31

Till You Walk in Her Shoes   32

Mist   33

On Horseback   34

Things I Wish I'd Asked My Big Sister   36

Three

Cordelia   41

Words   42

Advice to Modern Spies   43

Infinity Everywhere   44

Young Blood   45

Enlightenment?   47

Pope Says Internet Is Gift from God   48

Error   49

Something Is Wrong   50

Hourglass   52

Thesaurus   53

True, Pleasant, and Necessary   54

Hearing Chamber Music   55

We Pre-Boomers   57

Four

Losing Touch   61

The Coat   62

Taking Out the Garbage   63

Yiddish   64

The Grandfather   65

Cookies Foretell a Refreshing Change   66

Miss Darlene's Dancing School   67

Surprise   69

Pretty Maids All in a Row   70

The Doctor and His Dog   71

How the Mighty Have Fallen   72

Professor Donato   73

Leaving   74

So They Are Not Alone   75

Notes   77

Acknowledgments   79

NO WAY OUT
BUT THROUGH

One

Veronica Lake

The dream was a lattice of intricate design,
a labyrinth, leaved, layered
like an incomprehensible plot.
She climbed the lattice steadily though half
blind, sensing the shape of the slats imported
from Brazil, land of exotic flora,
facelifts, favelas. Oh Ipanema, she cried,
murmuring the song, then woke
to drab daylight sifting through the slats.
She tried to slip through the lattice, catch the dream
on the fly but daylight gripped her in its teeth.
She entreated sleep: let me stay
forever in that arbor of gaudy ripeness.
Let me hear the silky whisper of the dahlias
and narcissus, suck their nectar, taste
what the bees taste, I'd even eat the bees,
so sweet and pungent, lick their fuzz and be
transformed, Veronica Lake I'll call myself,
slender and draped in sheets of honeyed hair
like billowing sails on a sea of blossoms.

Collecting Myself

What flawed vision made me buy the book
of bilingual Russian stories, page three turned down
a year now, something by Gogol—
traveler, inn, horse, the rest a blur;
the costly binoculars, the high-heeled pumps
that pinched even in the store, the eyeliner
I can't apply, with one eye blind.
Monocular me.

All of it useless: I'd need different eyes,
different feet, a different self altogether,
one who reads Russian fluently and sees
a properly dimensioned world,
showing what my flat sight denies,
the fabled depths.

The Ladders

I was climbing risky rope ladders,
slowly, step by step, nearing the topmost rung
of the topmost ladder, it was some sort of quest.
I knew the reward was waiting at the peak.

Then sleep ejected me, the landscape shrank
like a spot of light imploding, the dream
unraveling like a seam joining two worlds,
though a trace of honeysuckle hung in the air
and my hands still stung from the prickly ropes.
What I sought wasn't a thing but a place. Somewhere
to go home to, where I'd never been.

Night after night I plunge into sleep
braced for the climb, the wobbly rungs,
the rough ropes searing my soles and palms.
I will know what I seek when I reach it.

Nocturnal Repertory

I'm summoned to a dinner in Jerusalem
to help the parties settle their dispute,
but packing is such a drag . . . What to wear?
Why not go bowling instead?

I've grown accustomed to my nighttime larks:
The room darkens. A still of expectation.
The curtain rises on the dreamer's follies:
Trains, of course, and sky-high escalators.
Daredevil leaps on skis and snowmobiles,
the recital for which I'm utterly unprepared . . .

Some nights my dead drop by, they're looking well,
they linger over coffee in the kitchen,
then say their time is up, like Cinderella.
They've hardly gone when a tsunami sweeps in
while I stand watching from a balcony.
Voices call me—Run! But I watch and wait.

I feast to bursting using golden chopsticks.
Can you gain weight from what you eat in dreams?
Are orgasms real when they happen in dreams? I mean,
you feel them but are they really happening?
Or . . . what do I mean?

Waking obliterates the show. Still,
I'm swaddled in the feel of it, the mood,
a sensation matching no sense organ,
no more substantial than
a soap bubble sailing down my bloodstream.

Is sleep presenting me with gifts, to hoard
until the words return? Or rather leaving me a sack
of junk to carry on my back?

Forgetting

Absence rarely makes the heart grow fonder,
or so my mother said, popping a blackberry
into her mouth—we'd raided the patch
at the far edge of the woods. Absence, she said,
begets forgetting. And while you mightn't so swiftly
forget a blackberry's taste or a thorn's prick,
or a cloud's sheep shape you spied skimming
low like a darning needle over a lake,
how fast
the lineaments of face or voice or touch
vanish,
Like that! She snapped
her fingers, bolted down the berry.

First Loves

The first was Richie with freckles and a voice
oddly raspy for our age, which was six.
A witty boy who laughed a lot; his freckles
pulsed with humor. We walked to school
hand in hand. He grew up to manage
a Las Vegas casino, and as rumor had it,
dealt drugs on the side. Not suitable at all,
for the long haul. I can see us hand in hand,
making our slow way down East New York Avenue,
looking both ways at every corner, finally reaching
the schoolyard and darting to our respective lines.
This was true love, if brief. But all through high school,
meeting in the halls, we greeted each other warmly,
sweet ripples of intimacy and affection
coursing between us.

The next was a girl, Paula. I was nine.
It was her name that drew me, so exotic,
so different from the names of my daily friends,
the Barbaras, Carols, Judys, and Susans of Brooklyn.
Paula came from afar, somewhere upstate, and spent
her school vacations with her uncle and aunt
across the street. Distance too was exotic.
I craved the exotic; my father mocked me for the word.
I asked him once if he ever longed to travel,
maybe to Europe. I've been to Europe, he snarled.
He left Russia at twelve, abandoning
the yellow armband he had to wear to school.
Also exotic was Paula's skin, brown like an Indian
or Mexican though she was neither, most likely
descended from the Sephardim of the Middle East.
Whenever my mother announced, Paula's here,
I rushed across the street to ring her bell.
I didn't know then that I was in love.

We sat on my bed, with legs crossed,
dressing paper dolls or simply talking,
the way girls of nine, like women, love to do.
After a year or two she stopped coming.
Paula, wherever you are,
I missed you so.

Thirteen, a bad year for any girl.
We summered in the Catskills, a site of torpor
worse even than Brooklyn, and shared a porch
with the family next door.
Of the two sons who worked in the day camp,
it was the older boy, nineteen, I craved,
as girls so often fix on the unattainable.
Large and dark like Paula, black hair,
crew cut, a ruddy, good-natured face umarred
by thought or introspection.
He always wore bathing trunks; I stared
at his tanned body and his hairy legs.
For some forgotten reason he called me Tex,
I thrilled to the name. One day I sat on my porch
in my bathing suit, holding my towel, hoping
he'd appear. And, miracle, his screen door opened,
out he came in his trunks, carrying a towel.
Hi, Tex. His voice sliced a path through my innards.
I can conjure that slicing feeling to this day.
Going to the pool? I nodded. Me too, he said.
Come walk with me. Indescribable joy,
walking down the dirt road with Lenny,
hoping my friends would see us.
It was almost like a date.

Maybe from that day on we'd be a couple,
like the many transient couples the summer shaped—
only coupledom could ease the seeping boredom—
those little loves that ended at Labor Day.
But when we reached the pool, he joined his friends
and I joined mine. I'd been imagining
some horseplay in the water, or tossing a ball.
I relived that five-minute walk all through the summer
and the deadly fall.

Some years later I married a boy, not
my preferred lumberjack type. I loved him anyway.
I imagined he was taller than he was.
We talked on the phone at night for hours,
I in the bedroom I'd inherited
when my sister left to get married, as every girl
had to do eventually. I was amazed
that a boy could actually converse
and read books. I didn't discover till later
that such boys were plentiful
if you had the patience to wait and knew where to look.
It was like buying the first house that you see,
and sometimes that works out quite well.
I love him but as we grow old I often wonder
how I could have plunged so thoughtlessly,
blind-eyed, into the future with a stranger
I found in a theater, and other times
it seems a stroke of luck, miraculous.

Hard and Soft

She won't soften, he won't harden.
She, harder of heart, calls him a bleeding heart.
He, warm-hearted, if hardly bloody,
won't judge her harshly although he's aware
what she cares for is her art. She keeps herself
apart, austere, while he studies how to ease
the pain of sufferers in foreign parts.

In bed, with hearts and bodies bare,
he is quite hard enough, knows how to please
with gentle art. At times she imagines a lover
more daring, until she feels the blare
of pleasure, and more pleasure to spare.
Her greedy heart beats to his loving care,
his satisfying hardness.

                   When they argue, at the start
she declares her views too heartily, while he
seeks not to gain the point but, mild and sane,
takes the measure of her argument.
Reason goes against her grain. His fairness
drives her to despair. Despite the strain,
enchained, heart to heart, they remain.

What the Poets Never Write about Love

The actual words murmured: not
Ah, your silken thighs, your breasts
like tender hills, but, Shit,
my zipper's stuck. My arm
is getting numb, please move. Wait,
I'll do the sleeve, and no, it hooks
in front not back. Hold on a sec,
I have a hair in my mouth, and move your ass,
I can't breathe this way. Remember,
I asked you once before to cut your fingernails?
Not to rush you or anything but
I can't stay in this fucking position another minute.

This act they say displays our animal nature
yet we're not, after all, like animals in love,
who finish, pant, grunt, saunter off.
They do not lie together after, or kiss,
laughing at their words of love, awkward
intimacies of bodies getting in their own way
on the tumbling, humbling path to bliss.

The German Class

I am the teacher.
The students are surly and suspicious.
They sense my German is inadequate.
Every day I forget the German class,
remembering only when the hour is nearly up.
I rush, run, but as in all dreams,
can't find the room. Up and down stairs
panting, peering, imploring everyone I pass.
At last I arrive. The students are studying their phones.
I rush to the desk, start the lesson: a passage
from Flaubert. They're quick to remind me
this is the German class and not the French.

The students have morphed into four-year-olds.
They play with a train set,
sending it zigging and zagging round the tracks.
What can they possibly care about Flaubert,
his fevered quests for *le mot juste.*
I myself don't care for varnished perfection.
If only they'd sit down I'd teach them a song,
"Lili Marlene," all I know of German.
Suddenly they approach, waving
their menacing little tracks like sticks.

Deliverance: the bell rings and they flee.
Next night, same story. Surely I'll be fired. I vow
to get to class on time and be prepared.
Still, time after time I'm late, can't find the room,
the students are surly and suspicious. . . .

Namesake

In the shadow of Our Lady's cathedral
where Hugo's hunchback clanged the iron bells,
the Café Esmeralda's brisk with trade,
waiters skimming like insects over water,
their trays of quivering confections held aloft.
The enervated tourists study maps.
Meanwhile, outside, the ragged gypsy girl
sits mute on the baking pavement,
slitted eyes, toothpick legs outstretched,
palm cupped for handouts. She's inert
like the grimy statues of saints across the way.
A vast indifference clouds her like a caul,
or a grim bell waiting to be struck,
iron colder than the indifference of the crowd.

A Dress Laments

I was thrilled when you found me in the thrift shop,
so dim and dingy, I longed for rescue.
Others had tried me on but I felt no rapport.
I'd develop awkward folds and bumps
till they tossed me to the floor in frustration,
where I lay crumpled till someone brushed me off
and hung me up.

But when I felt you fingering me, testing
the texture of my fabric, I had an inkling
we'd make a good pair: Your shape
would fill out mine, confer a shape,
while mine would outline yours to perfection.
In your closet I found elegant
and courteous companions,

but quickly I became the favorite.
We looked so fine, your silver brooch against
my inky surface. Nights, we went gallivanting—
how long since I'd been flaunted on the town!
I believe you truly loved me, for a time.
You never tossed me rudely on a chair.
You patiently removed the wax

from a candle at your lover's birthday party. . . .
How different from my former owner—months
closeted, freed only for formal dinners.
But just as I was reveling in my triumphs,
you changed. I was supplanted by newer,
less clingy items. Was it the change of lovers
or the ten unwanted pounds?

I tried my best to drape you to conceal them,
but there's only so much a dress can do. . . .
You knew that too, you felt a pang at parting.
I hate to sound resentful but you might
have passed me to a slimmer friend. Instead
you brought me to another shabby shop,
consigned to the worst fate: Beauty unseen,

unrecognized—a kind of death for a dress,
as well as the woman inside it. How much longer
can I keep shuttling from body to body
before I lose my luster? Even the most
meticulously fashioned black silk sheath
can't halt the moldering of time,
any more than the woman who wears it.

A Bad Rap

I've always been partial to the fisherman's wife—
those outlandish dreams—
the one who made her husband scatter wishes
on the magic flounder fished up from the sea.
Instead of a hovel she craved a modest cottage.
Granted! But the woman was insatiable.

On and on with her demands.
A royal palace didn't suffice, she wanted
dominion over the earth, the heavens, no less—
Queen, Empress, God!
For such presumption she was dumped
back in her hovel
to become a cautionary tale
for greedy children.

Pity the poor suffering dreamers,
wracked with desire for all the world can offer.
If not for that overripe imagination
some of us share, she'd have been spared.
She'd have been content with a modern kitchen,
designer clothes, a flashy car, and be remembered
as an exemplary woman. Only grandeur
was denied her. Power.

The Two Supers

The Puerto Rican super next door
was an outrageous flirt, and I,
in a careless way, flirted back.
I couldn't take a super seriously.
When he asked me to dinner
I thanked him but declined.
He looked downcast.
Maybe in another life, I said,
meaning to be kind.
Indelible, the hurt look on his face.
From that day on he never spoke to me
and turned away when I passed.
No way to swallow back the clumsy phrase.
When he left, I felt relieved.

The new super was Luis. No flirting,
just friendly talk. He likes to say
I haven't changed in thirty years.
I like to hear it, laugh and say it back,
we laugh together standing on the street.
I push my granddaughter in her stroller,
Luis leans down to greet her,
reaches in his pocket for his harmonica,
plays "My Darling Clementine."
She jiggles her arms and legs in time,
gazes at him in dazzlement,
as if she hears the music of the spheres.
Indelible, the glee that's on her face.
Almost enough to erase
that other face.

Renée Returned

It happened with Renée, that uncanny likeness,
you see someone on the street from long ago,
you almost rush over—wait, impossible,
she'd have aged thirty years, the same as you.

Yet there she is miraculously striding
down Lexington Avenue, reborn, *renée*,
young, blond, translucent-seeming skin,
her dancer's lithe gait, and you can't help thinking

maybe she never turned on the gas after all,
and maybe her mother never telephoned
to tell you the news, sounding more angry than stricken,
and maybe you needn't have felt so guilty

because you hadn't a clue about how to help
thirty years ago, though you did take her in
when she called at midnight with no place to go,
but even in your ignorance of madness,

you knew enough not to leave the children
alone with her. You stayed up nights
in the dim kitchen, hearing her weird stories,
ravings—she'd always talked disjointedly—

uncertain what was true and what imagined,
while she lit matches one by one and tossed them,
burning, into the overflowing ashtray,
sometimes missing. When at last you slept

you dreamed of fire and feared for your husband and children,
so you sent her away despite your long friendship
and her luminescent smile and how
she danced like a levitating white-limbed nymph,

and never heard a word of her for years
until her mother's call. You'd like to approach
that beautiful stranger, her look-alike, and say . . .
But you could never find the proper words.

Trans

I was supposed to be born a giraffe,
with a gorgeous patchy coat,
chocolate islands in a creamy sea,
and stilty legs so that I walk
like I'm wearing high heels for the first time,
stepping with tremulous deliberation,
taller than any creature on four legs or two,
and when I bend to drink from the stream
my body traces a supple parabola,
and I have a gentle nature,
peace-loving, and an air of tranquil confidence.

I knew from my earliest years
that I was assigned to the wrong body. Once,
I saw an orange fox staring at me
from the edge of the woods and thought
she might be summoning me to join her,
but I was mistaken, her gaze was far too sharp,
her face too angular.
I've wondered if I should have been a fish—
whenever I see a body of water,
I'm drawn to jump in,
but a fish is cold and damp and scaly.

My skin wants to be bare and dry under a hot sun
and I must eat green leaves off high branches
and care for gawky young ones made in my image.
I'm waiting for science to alter this outer lie
I occupy
and give my misplaced nature its rightful shape.

Stitching Skin

I'm out of my skin, six layers scraped off,
only the innermost left,
too tender for this weather.
Skin can't be bought, it's do-it-yourself—
days stitching petals, fragrant, flexible.
The work is slow:

precise articulation of the toes,
curve of heel and calf, the complex
folds and holes of the sexual parts,
the tilt of breasts, knobs of collarbone,
sloping vales of earlobes.

At last it's ready to wear. I climb in:
Fits like a glove.
With exposure the petals will grow tough,
rough to the touch, resistant
to all varieties of weather,
and willing to wither.

Two

For Beverly

Reduced

They gouged your mouth out, carved it up like meat,
but left the brain intact. You know it all.
Did the surgeon's knife weep as it sliced the roots
of teeth, the cankered rot of tender tissue?

They can't restore your fine-tuned powers of speech,
make your hollowed out ears hear, your blind
eyes see the wind lifting the leaves
beyond your window. Oh, what will make you rise

from your forever chair and swim again,
loping from the lake, your velveteen bathing suit,
your burnished hair, your movie-star smile
in love with life, drops spraying. On screen,

you lope toward the camera, bound
across the tennis court, pedal
on the tandem bike, skim over ice,
all the things you taught me how to do.

You were the big sister. Now
I simply stroke your hands.

No Way Out but Through

I know I have to die, but not today,
my sister's joke, her every morning mantra,
when she was old, before the thorn took hold.

When we find people dead in their bed we say,
at least it was easy, they died in their sleep.
For all we know they were wide awake, gasping,

rasping, panicky, choking alone.
Why call for help? Nothing can stop it.
Only let it be quick, and quickly done.

In wretched times we say this too shall pass.
But how to get through now? How to leap
over it to a future, or to none?

No way out but through. You have to live it.
You have to live it. Later her mantra changed:
I know I have to die, so let it be today.

Dayyenu

The body knows enough
to recognize the moment of enough
as when the doctor said
three months to live and
Have you any questions?
I want to go home
she murmured through her excavated mouth.
Our brother maneuvered her into the car,
a heavy weight though she was hollowed out
inside, a weighty hollow.
And so to bed where she performed
the one act she could manage on her own,
laid down and died.
Enough of this, her body told the world,
thanks, but that will do. Dayyenu.

Till You Walk in Her Shoes

I'm walking in your shoes, the black boots trimmed
in fur, found in your closet, price tag dangling,
the evening of the day we buried you.

I was rooting around to get a feel of the clothes.
None would fit, but maybe a scent remained
in the satiny stuff I pressed to my face.

I opened the boxes of shoes. A perfect fit,
those boots you never walked in. Still, I feel
what you'd have felt, wearing them. A long

weighty sadness, solitude, but buoyancy
too, tough soles willing to keep on walking
through the thick dark of the path ahead.

Sisters know things about each other
no other knows, how the blood feels as it flows,
how the breath feels livening the muscles,

the trail of linked thoughts, the bubble
of laughter in the throat. I'm walking, knowing
you. I'm walking in your shoes.

Mist

Of all she taught me I like best the lore
of spray-on cologne. Forget, she said,
the dabbing at wrists and collarbone.
Spray a column of air in front of you
then walk through it, preferably naked.
Walk through the mist. The mist will cling to you.

I sprayed the air and ventured through the mist,
a sweet fleeting pleasure, like a brief kiss,
or an instant in a tropical jungle,
or in the juicy heart of a flower.
A minuscule light shower of scented rain.

I suspect she was speaking in metaphor,
some lesson about life I can't decipher.
I want it to signify something, like an heirloom
with a tale attached. Something to unwrap
from time to time and contemplate.

But all she's left me is a fragrant mist
that shapes itself to my skin, a shower
of scented particles that cling.

On Horseback

I was going to your house on horseback,
not the new house where you suffered
and rode the stairs in a magic chair,
but your old house with the lake and beach in back,
where we swam away the summer afternoons
breathing in the scent of ripe tomatoes
from the garden next door.

I hadn't been on a horse in years and though
this one was small and docile,
it was hard to navigate the city streets.
Crossing the George Washington Bridge was perilous,
the river below dizzying, so dark and broad.
Merging onto the Palisades, I was scared,
so was the horse, he trembled and I soothed him
with pats and gentle words. Cautious,
we stayed in the right lane.

The horse must have taken a wrong turn for soon
we were trotting through a string of villages.
A cop stopped us and warned
I'd have to pick up speed once on the Thruway
or I'd hold up traffic. He dispatched a fellow officer
to ride with us and act as guide.
Our guide said we'd be crossing several rivers.
How so? I asked. I wasn't going far,
only to Spring Valley, to my sister's old house,
for remembrance.

The wind of our galloping stole my words.
The guide went on as if I hadn't spoken.
You must cross Acheron, the river of sorrow, he said,
and Kokytos, the river of lamentation.
Those rivers I knew well.
I've crossed them already, I protested,
when my sister was dying.
You must cross them again, he said, and led the way.

Again I passed through the rivers of sorrow
and lamentation, my poor horse laboring on
with water up to his mane, but at the last crossing,
Lethe, the river of forgetfulness,
he refused to budge. Turn back, he whispered,
but I paid no heed, he was only a horse,
and I spurred him on.

After Lethe, the land was sere, crazed
like a shattered mirror. The horse stumbled,
the guide had deserted us. I forgot
where I was going, and why.

Things I Wish I'd Asked My Big Sister

Did you ever get Mom's recipe for that soup
we called football soup because she told
our brother it would make him big and strong
like a football player?

What did they say about my damaged eye
when I was born?
Did it bother them a lot? Or not,
since there'd been three miscarriages before me,
so what if I wasn't perfect?

When she told you she couldn't bear his screaming
and wished she could get a divorce,
what did you say? Did you encourage her?
Knowing you, I bet you told her to endure it.
Did he shout as much when you were growing up?
Did it frighten you the way it frightened me?

Why did they never have my crooked tooth
straightened? Your teeth were so perfect.
Did you ever wear braces?

You told me she was depressed for a year
after her older brother died
and the aunts took care of you.
So how did she get over it?

And how come you never kept in touch with the cousins
you grew up with in the brownstone in Williamsburg
during the Depression,
one family on each floor?

Why were you angry when she cleaned up your kitchen?
I liked it when she cleaned up my kitchen.

What was it like when she roller skated with you?
I can't imagine her roller-skating.
What did she look like thin and lithe?

That day we were talking about feminism
and you said when you got cranky
your husband screwed you to the bed,
did you really mean that?
Tell me you didn't mean it.

Three

Cordelia

It's always irked me, her sanctimonious muteness,
essence of nothing, the crucial word.
The pure, self-satisfied, and favored daughter,
refusing to bend an inch, not even to spare

the old man the torments of his folly.
She treasures principle and reeks of purity,
she can't endure an insult to her pride.
She coddles her stiffened soul, she savors

that chilling negativity. True,
she's the instrument of Lear's lesson.
But for Cordelia he'd stay ignorant
of raw need. What irony she wreaks

to teach a haughty king humility,
she, who refuses to be humbled.

Words

Can you grasp a floral poem
if you've never seen a garden?
A poem about music if you've never heard
a piano's slippery riffs?

I like to think that words,
by their long and faithful service,
assume the scents and shapes,
the qualities and quiddities,
of what they represent,
like the velveteen rabbit,
who through longing and patience
and being loved, turned real.

Words that are cherished overcome
abstraction: foxglove, verbena, rue,
dahlia, poppy, jonquil, and nasturtium
pleasure the ear as well as eye.
Oboe, tympani, trombone, cello, flute
sound upon the page as well as stage.
So the blind can listen to the garden,
the hard of hearing see the symphony.

Advice to Modern Spies

The Greeks, I read somewhere, had a neat way
to transmit secrets no technology
could intercept. The messenger's head was shaved,
the message written on his naked scalp.
He made the trip on foot and it was long,
long enough to grow a head of hair.
Once he arrived they shaved his head anew
and gathered round to read the secret text,
then scrubbed it clean and inked a brief reply.
The illiterate messenger shuttled to and fro,
not knowing what his head foretold:
ancestral voices prophesying war.

Infinity Everywhere

Ungraspable, yet we're encoded in its riddle,
as in this instant's glance
at the first of the cherry blossoms
this April out of infinite Aprils,
this glance out of all the possible glances
at possible blossoms. The sun's rays
slant through the leaves at this ephemeral angle,
of all the angles yet to slant before the fall
of dark. Or as in music, the finite scale
yielding a plenitude of melodies
and if one note is altered,
a different melody.
One more brush stroke on a Rothko painting,
itself a canvas of infinity, would show
another of the countless hues of the single rainbow.
One shift of limb in sleeping lovers' embrace
shapes another of the unending embraces
in love's infinity.

Young Blood

New York Times, 5/4/2014: "Two teams of scientists published studies . . .
showing that blood from young mice reverses aging in old mice, rejuvenat-
ing their muscles and brains. . . . Experts said that [the research] could lead
to treatments for disorders like Alzheimer's disease and heart disease."

What works for decrepit mice
might work for us:
a newfound paradise.
How fabulous

to live safely immune
to age and pain,
disease inopportune
wrecking our brain,

casting its somber pall.
So science dreams
of fresh young blood for all,
abundant streams.

But who could raise the cash
except the rich,
who'd do it in a flash.
There lies the glitch.

Here as everywhere,
Inequity,
in meting out such dear
longevity.

Perhaps we could engage
the unemployed
and pay a decent wage
for blood deployed.

Rejuvenation, thus,
the next frontier.
The rich we'll always have with us.
Mice, prepare.

Enlightenment?

I've heard of the Buddhists' stun of satori,
transformative, or so they say. I'm tempted,
but I'm not one for lotused meditation,
wouldn't relish some passing Master
striking me with a stick.

Still, I felt it once, something like it anyway,
at fourteen, having completed the agony
of being thirteen, walking down Montgomery Street
from the subway, approaching the sharp turn
onto East New York Avenue in dusk, in spring,
a peculiar grayish light like dust draining
down: all at once the world was perfect
all things precisely as they should be, my place
within all things precisely right. I knew myself
as what I was and always would be.
The street was aglow as if back lit. No void
but fullness brimming at the horizon's rim.
I gave a glad assent to all I saw.
This lasted just a moment. Once I crossed
the street it fell away. I was unchanged,
no mystic bath of wisdom or of goodness,
except I knew such things could happen.

Pope Says Internet Is Gift from God

In the beginning, it must have been, on that idle
seventh day, a break from the serious work
of teasing skies and seas and space
out of the void. To pass the time,
he conjured cyberspace, curious
at how we'd plunder it, our greedy hands,
nullity sifting through our fingers.

It waited hidden for millennia
in some dank cavern, long before the first
fish clambered gasping to the shore,
until the scientists unearthed it,
bored after the in-your-face bomb, seeking
a trinket more intricate, with digital
straitjacket, an open maw starved for data,
tyrannical as a newborn howling to be fed.

From it they fashioned a parallel world, the flip
side of that first green and blue creation.
How it enfolds us, the stench of waste
rimming every space, the very air
wikified. It gulps up time
like those vacuum cleaners, holes in the wall,
that swallow all the dirt in the room,
never needing to be emptied.

Error

The message on the screen was jarring:
"The following configuration
is in an error state. Pay urgent attention
to this matter."

I clicked for Help: is a state of error
anything like a state of sin?
I'm not remorseful but for a curious
tiptoeing in the chest,

burden in the gut. Of what crime
is my configuration guilty?
Is my state reversible? Which button?
Undo, repair, retry?

Something makes me doubt I'll ever see
the blessed message of exoneration:
"The system has recovered
from a serious error."

Something Is Wrong

Marcus Jelinek, our college roommate,
had the neatest of desks, the surface nearly bare,
books in even stacks, pens in a mug.
Marcus was always setting things in order,
straightening papers, careful to make sure
nothing was touching any other thing.
At home, in his closet, he said, no garment
or hanger ever touched another.
Our closet was too crowded for such scruples.

The foods on his plate at mealtime couldn't touch.
Meat, rice, vegetables, in discrete heaps.
When he wasn't looking, we pushed his rice
and vegetables together, blurring the borders.
He fixed his plate straightaway,
and if it couldn't be done, he tossed it out.

Whenever I caught him fussing at his desk
he'd look abashed and say, Hey,
just putting things in order. This was his passion.

You'll never get your world exactly right,
I said. Life is disorder. Perhaps, said Marcus,
but I do what I can. Wherever I look
I find something awry. Wrong-headedness
and muddle. Ignorance and malice
ending in mayhem. No better within—
every thought bleeds into every other,
no notion or emotion clear or pure.
It helps to set the desk to rights, at least.

Later I came to know what Marcus meant:
Our composition was blundered, the patterns of mind
and heart disjointed, shifting endlessly
like colored bits attempting to correct
a flawed mosaic or botched tapestry,
the stitches veering every which way.
Marcus could never speak of this precisely,
the nature of the matter being so unstable,
nor can I.

Hourglass

Turn the hourglass over,
give it some exercise, he said,
unless you want this moment to go on
forever.

Thesaurus

I'm in love, that is, smitten, with M. Roget.
Not one of those ardent obsessive loves
that shred the heart, nor a love that longs
to be requited, acknowledged, or appreciated,
but a love that gives comfort and consolation,
smooths the ruffled brow of care,
tempers the wind to the shorn lamb,
and lays the flattering unction to the soul.

M. Roget's endearingly tidy mind
banishes the chaos of language, he's tossed it
to the winds, to the dogs, overboard. He sorts, sifts,
sieves, and systematizes the lexicon,
gathers every arcane synonym,
including all clichés and idioms,
into a flawless taxonomy. He cleaves
the world into categories from which nothing—
absolutely, reliably, unerringly nothing—
is omitted, from Abstract Relations, to Space, Matter,
Intellect, Volition, and Affections.

Only that last, Affections—if I may venture
a suggestion, even an admonitory
word—might be ranked more highly
in the hierarchy, *viz. to wit*,
prioritized.

True, Pleasant, and Necessary

Somewhere I read this rule: to be discreet,
don't speak unless your words can meet
two of the following three criteria:
Pleasant, true, and necessary.

Think of all the truths the rule precludes,
being neither pleasant nor necessary:
I loved my lover more than I love you.
I hate it when you act just like your father.
Your brother was the favorite. You
were the unwanted child, the accident.
How to judge which truths we need to vent?
Some are like letters better left unsent.

Who can manage such a stringent rule,
with every smoothing self-protective fib,
or glib and pleasant needless lie
stuck forever in the throat?
Only a saint or a fool.

Hearing Chamber Music

The longer I study the lanky violist, the stronger
grow my suspicions that he's wearing a wig.
A splendid head of hair, white
as a bride's satin gown, straight, stray
wisps falling over his forehead,
tossing just so at turbulent or tender moments
in the Beethoven quartet, *Il Serioso*.
The thing with wigs that gives them away is the part,
or the lack of part, how you can't see scalp
between the parts
parted by the part.

The hair of the others is nondescript, although
the cellist has a puckish cut
that arrows down his forehead, imparting
to his round face a cherubic air:
cherubic cellist.

All four have glossy black shoes that glint
in the stage lights, and suddenly an upward phrase
in the Beethoven pierces my skin,
shifts my heart in its chamber,
turns my blood the colors of the rainbow.
I'm gliding on the notes that float
on sweet tranquil air
and I remember why I'm here:

Because beauty alone can save me,
I've always known, so I go seeking it.
This is what salvation feels like:
untethered, catapulted into joy.

They stop, arc their bows through the air
with controlled slowness. The movement is over.
In the pause I cling to the feeling, fast dispersing.
For a little while I was saved.

We Pre-Boomers

All through college we commiserated:
How much we had to do!

Today I got a lot done, we'd announce,
or, I couldn't get anything done. The habit
stuck like glue.

Grown now, we ask each other, Did you manage
to get much done? Or have you still
a great deal left to do?

As if we had a mission to fulfill.
So occupied, we never dreamed what more
we might pursue,

or learned the cunning of how not to do.
Time spooled away in the fret of doing. Carve
on my tombstone: She got an awful lot done.

Four

Losing Touch

I'm losing touch with my mother. She used to come
whenever I called, her round face crowned
by fuzzy orange curls, a loop of flame.
She floated in mid-air, smiling. Gone
were the anxious furrows. What she had feared
had happened and the fear died with her.

                    I never asked
about the place she'd traveled from.
I sensed it was a subject out of bounds.
Instead I asked for favors—even now,
the selfish child. She was the generous one:
when I admired her strands of bright green beads,
she took them off her neck to place on mine.

                    So I'd ask, Ma,
make certain good things happen for my children.
She nodded as if trusted with a mission
and drifted off. Sometimes she succeeded:
the good things happened.

                    But lately she comes rarely,
as if she's sliding farther into the ether,
or maybe I've stopped calling for her, stopped
wanting or caring about those certain things,
content to let life happen on its own. Still,
I miss those visitations, the rosy face,
the hair aflame.

The Coat

I felt such love for the coat. Mostly I think
for the hood, whose fake fur
feathered my cheeks. The coat was plaid,
dark green, red, black; it reached my knees.
In it I felt bigger than I was,
eight years old with clumsy leather leggings.
I hated those, and the squishy galoshes.

The first day I wore the coat I made an igloo
with Ruthie and Joyce and Eleanor. The snow
was two days old, perfect for packing. We made
a splendidly arched entrance to crawl in.
The igloo was just large enough for two
if we kept our knees scrunched up.
We took turns sitting in it, two by two.

Long after the day began to fade
and the other mothers fetched my friends to supper
I stayed in the gleaming igloo all alone,
blinking at the white dazzle,
my humble pleasure dome of ice, so bright
though the light outside was graying fast.
I took my mitten off to stroke the ceiling,

happy in my perfect coat and perfect igloo,
I could stay crouched in it forever.
But soon my mother appeared, scolding:
What was I doing sitting in the cold,
was I crazy, I'd just got over scarlet fever.
I couldn't explain I wasn't cold
but warmer than I had ever felt indoors.

Taking Out the Garbage

Picture a graying middle-aged man,
white shirt, sleeves rolled up, tie loosened,
still in his good trousers from the working day.
As lavender twilight descends like a sheer scrim
over Brooklyn's brick row houses, he stands
in his driveway beside the metal garbage can,
one foot firmly on the pavement, the other
high in the air, about to descend into the can.

He stomps on the paper bag he just deposited.
He stomps his foot on the garbage hard, merciless,
over and over. Take that, you pillaging Cossacks,
you Jew-hating animals delighting in pogroms,
who grafted on our arms the yellow band, take that,
you gougers who made us pay in blood for schooling,
who tossed my brother into the ditch at Babi Yar.
Take that, and that! This
is my father, the human compactor.

Yiddish

Only the old ones spoke it all the time and perfectly,
like Esther with the upswept white-yellow hair,
who scraped walnut shells from the afternoon's gossip
off the oilcloth table top with a butter knife
and at the edge tipped them into her waiting palm.

Yiddish, I thought, was something that happened to you
as you aged, like pink wrinkled cheeks and yellow-white
hair—I once saw it gleaming down her back at midnight,
as she stood at the top of the stairs in her flannel nightgown.

The older you were, the better you spoke. It grew on you.
My parents could speak it too but only now and then,
for secrets, and not with Esther's deep old-world gargle.
My older sister spoke it with a new-world accent—
I trusted that would fade over the years—and I,
still a child, though I understood their Yiddish,
could utter just a few phrases that made people laugh.
I didn't mind, I knew I'd improve with time
and when I was truly old but straight-backed and beautiful
like Esther, my voice would be hoarse
and would acquire the old-world gargle,
and from my tongue would flow a consummate Yiddish,
a lifetime's worth of perfecting.

The Grandfather

The grandfather, the famed geneticist, retired,
is swimming deep inside his inscrutable,
unscrutinized self, like a fish seeking shelter.
All his life he preferred
the kaleidoscope of the chromosomes
to the unmeasurable ripples within.
Now his shoulders are curved, his head lowered,
eyes straining as if to peer into his heart.

His handwriting, still sternly vertical,
is narrowing, illegible, the letters cramped,
leaning on each other like a row of tenements,
his voice so soft we need to ask, What?

He's well, still reads his daily paper thoroughly,
takes long ruminative walks with the ancient dog,
scans the scientific journals, laughs at jokes,
all the while drifting in the depths,
seeking what he is made of.

He keeps the world at bay while he traces
the neglected mazes, the obscure spiraling
of self, tangled like a mandrake root,
lichened and cobwebbed from disuse,
his final research.

Cookies Foretell a Refreshing Change

Success is being at peace with yourself.
You have an ability to sense and know a higher truth.
Your flair for the creative has an important place
in your life. You are very expressive
and positive in words, acts, and feelings.
Never compare yourself to the best others
can do, but to the best you can do.

A refreshing change is in your future: Your talents
will be recognized and suitably rewarded.
You will reach the highest possible point
in your business or profession.
The secret of success is constancy of purpose.

A refreshing change is in your future.
An unexpected event will bring you riches:
You will inherit a large sum of money.
You will have an exciting business adventure.
Your income will increase.

A refreshing change is in your future:
You are about to embark on a most delightful journey.
You have the ability to adapt to diverse situations.
An unexpected relationship will become permanent.
The secret of success is being guided by cookies.

Miss Darlene's Dancing School

Miss Darlene, dark, slender, acne-scarred,
married next-door Marvin and came to share
his basement flat. Upstairs, his mother
claimed Miss Darlene had danced with the Rockettes.
She opened a dancing school a block away.
We girls on the block were conscripted to take lessons,
to help support the newly married couple.

We got shiny black patent leather shoes
with black ribbons and taps on heels and toes.
We danced to *East Side, West Side,*
all around the town. I can still perform
the opening bars today, but my lessons ended
at a step called the Buffalo, which I never mastered
because Miss Darlene's closed, she got pregnant.

That was postwar Brooklyn, known for dullness,
before the West Indians came with their bouncy speech
and the Jews in drear black coats and uglifying
wigs. Pre-chic Brooklyn, before the new
colonizers parked their double strollers
outside the bookstores and the restaurants
serving foods Miss Darlene had never heard of.

One scorching summer afternoon
I visited my old street. The West Indians
had adorned the porches with wrought iron curlicues
and painted the front doors in fanciful hues.
Children played in the street as we had done,
the parents on the stoops fanning themselves.
I was the only white person. Near the house

of the family who'd owned the funeral parlor—the hearse
in the driveway at the ready, a reminder—
stood a Mister Softee truck. I got in line.
A woman asked, What was I doing there?
I didn't say this was my childhood home, simply
that I wanted ice cream, and she said,
You must want it real bad, to come out here.

Surprise

Mrs. Katz across the street was so enormous,
her condition wasn't known until quite late.
The size of a Hotpoint refrigerator, she sat
on the front porch humming, fanning herself
with a hanky, legs spread wide, knees
like blue-veined hillocks. Mr. Katz, a butcher,
could carve two wives from her, I thought,
then bit my tongue for such a naughty thought.
Mrs. Katz lured the imagination to the lurid.

When her pregnancy was clear, astonishment
streaked across the block. How did he find it?
my father murmured. I didn't know what he meant.
And then there arrived Melissa of the white-gold curls,
a lissome child, her mother's darling,
who perched on the vast lap, dispensing joy.
And I, however clever, couldn't have imagined that.

Pretty Maids All in a Row

Three women, three generations, in a row,
each swathed in plastic from the neck to toe,
each seated in a leather salon chair,
docile, as gunk is spread all through their hair.

Each has her own attendant, an expert band,
raking through the heads with combs in hand:
the speckled grey, the brown, and then the child,
hair long like ribbons, fleecy gold and wild.

The spectacle might move a tender heart,
even recall idealized works of art,
like Renoir's multigenerational dreams
or Mary Cassatt's sweetly pastel scenes.

An image of family unity, how nice!
All three afflicted by the scourge of lice.

The Doctor and His Dog

The brisk young doctor, upright, proud,
walked his Yorkshire Terrier
three times a day, fair or foul.
The dog had to trot to keep in step.
His greeting, What's the good word?

With time misfortunes settled on him
like a row of speckled starlings on a cable.
His wife died in childbirth,
the child was palsied, speechless.
Mornings, a special bus arrived
for the ailing girl. Frail, she sat in her chair
as he maneuvered it up the ramp
and kissed her good-bye, every day
till she died. He and the dog
still walked together daily, slower.

Time clutched him in its claws
dug in with its beak and shook him so hard
he was bent over in half and so slow
that traffic learned to stop for him
and the aging dog, trailing behind.

Now he rides in a motorized chair.
Three times a day foul or fair,
the old dog walks the old man.
What's the good word? he says.

How the Mighty Have Fallen

Platinum-bleached Miss Romanoff, Tsarina
of bookkeeping, with layers of caked powder
on her sour, corpse-like face, a voice like shovels
scraping dirt off coffins, was my tormentor,
kept me at my desk engaged in combat
with the giant leather ledger
till assets and debits matched to the ultimate cent.

My revenge was musing on her ruined ancestors,
the Russian royal family shot to death
(first made to pose for a photo proving
they were still alive): Nicholas, Alexandra,
and their children, including the enigmatic
Anastasia, who'd reappear from time to time—
portrayed by Ingrid Bergman in the movie—

till the bodies were dug up and DNA
showed Anastasia dead without a doubt.
But for the Revolution twisting history,
Miss Romanoff, I imagine a distant kin,
could be a lady-in-waiting in taffeta,
rendezvousing with wealthy counts instead
of keeping accounts for a discount furniture store,

shriveled by her thwarted fate, spitting
bile on a girl who lacked her noble blood,
starting college, afraid to be late for class.
But I endured her with a silent glee.
She was bound for life to the leather ledger,
while I would stage my private revolution
and know a different kind of royalty.

Professor Donato

The cashier rolls her eyes at the clumsy old man,
who drops the detergent, fumbles with the fruit,
and is taking an age to count out his dollar bills.
She frowns at the line of waiting customers—I'm next—
shakes her head in her heartless and ignorant youth.

The old man, the very clumsy slow old man,
his clothes drooping from a bony frame,
seems not to register her scorn, or else
he is past caring, or even hearing.
I clench my fists so I don't strangle her:
The man who tries her patience is the once
commanding Professor Donato, carrying home
his small provisions, plums and bread and soap.

He taught me European history,
pacing the classroom with authority,
muscled chest filling his smart gray suit,
parsing the phases of the past, the wars
and alliances, the rise and fall of empires,
the atrocities, pacts, betrayals, and humiliations
far greater than his own, here, now,
his lectures like an opera, each era an aria,
his mellow voice caressing every theme.
I loved to watch him stride about or reach
his firm arm up to chalk the board.

I want to rescue him, to speak to him,
speak *for* him, shout his true identity,
but speech would just prolong the ugly scene,
and he is busy pocketing his change.
When I scan the busy street, he's disappeared,
leaving me guilty, furious at time,
crueler than a callow grocery clerk.

Leaving

No way out but through the gates
Flung open to our common fates.
No chance to flee. No frightened pleas
Can halt our end or change our dates.

Who said the gate was strait? It's wide
To fit the cringing throngs outside.
Some have fallen to their knees,
Others crouch, in vain, to hide.

No trace here of the sublime.
Memory regurgitates each crime.
Terror invades us by degrees.
We shriek for mercy: grant us time.

So They Are Not Alone

My mother pitied the fate of her Uncle Shmuel,
back in the old country,
murdered before he could marry, no descendants,
while his brothers and sisters, immigrants all,
were frantically fruitful and multiplied.
Whenever a member of the clan was pregnant,
my mother reminded them of childless Shmuel.
The name doesn't have to be Shmuel, she'd say,
I know that sounds too foreign, or even Samuel.
Just an *S* would do. So he's not all alone.

Imagine them, safe at last in the afterlife,
the Alters and Avigdors, Berels, Boruchs, and Mendels,
Velvels and Tzvis surrounded by their namesakes,
just the one letter, the alien names, the Victors,
Barrys and Allans and Marks,
the Tonys, Brians, and Brents, all of an age.

And the beautiful names of the women, Yael and Rivka,
Zissel, Malka, Batya and Chaya, Dalit and Shoshana.
At their feet sit Roxane and Betty, Zoe, Marianne,
Heidi, Diane, Sophie, and Yvonne.

There you will always find a ready welcome.
Amid the chattering clusters of namesakes,
Some few, like great-uncle Shmuel, sit alone.

NOTES

"Hard and Soft": Suggested by Brenda Shaughnessy's poem, "Artless," in *Our Andromeda*.

"Dayyenu," "enough," in Hebrew. The word is used in the Passover Haggadah; the Jews freed from slavery in Egypt thank God for his series of acts during and after their release, each verse of the passage ending with "dayyenu," that is, it would have been enough.

"Advice to Modern Spies," "ancestral voices prophesying war," from Coleridge's "Kubla Khan."

"Pope Says Internet Is Gift from God," *Catholic Herald*, 1/23/14.

"True, Pleasant, and Necessary": I remember reading this prescription in Carol Shields's novel, *The Stone Diaries*, but I've been unable to find it again.

ACKNOWLEDGMENTS

Some of the poems in the collection have been published in the following journals:

"Mist" and "Forgetting" in Narrative.com; "On Horseback" in *Bosque*; "Hourglass" in *Poet Lore*; "Till You Walk in Her Shoes" in *Salamander*; "Veronica Lake" in *Denver Quarterly*; "The Two Supers" and "How the Mighty Have Fallen" in Literallatte.com; "Renée Returned" in the *Harvard Review*; "Advice to Modern Spies" in *Southwest Review*; "Miss Darlene's Dancing School" in Cleaver.com.